Disney

Z·O·M·B·I·E·S

EASY PIANO COLLECTION

© 2022 Disney

ISBN 978-1-7051-7911-6

Visit Hal Leonard Online at
www.halleonard.com

World headquarters, contact:
Hal Leonard
7777 West Bluemound Road
Milwaukee, WI 53213
Email: info@halleonard.com

In Europe, contact:
Hal Leonard Europe Limited
1 Red Place
London, W1K 6PL
Email: info@halleonardeurope.com

In Australia, contact:
Hal Leonard Australia Pty. Ltd.
4 Lentara Court
Cheltenham, Victoria, 3192 Australia
Email: info@halleonard.com.au

ZOMBIES

ZOMBIES 2

ZOMBIES 3

FIRED UP
from *ZOMBIES*

Written by MITCH ALLAN
and NIKKI LEONTI EDGAR

Moderately fast

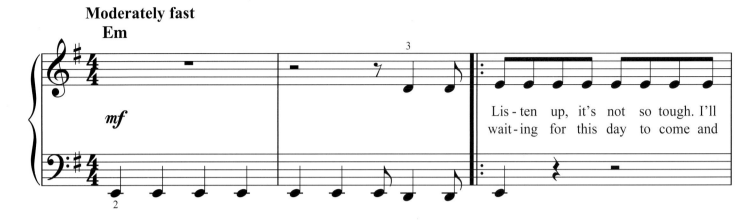

Lis - ten up, it's not so tough. I'll
wait - ing for this day to come and

tell you how it's done.   There's
it was all so clear.   Since I

real - ly noth - ing bet - ter than to
was a lit - tle girl I

hear you're num - ber one.   And
saw me stand - ing here.   And

I know how to get a crowd right
All the times they told me, "Walk a -

up and on their feet.   So,
way," I said, "For - get it."   I

if you want them in it,   I'll
knew where I was head - ed   and

show you how to get it.
I was gon - na get it.

Ain't no moun - tain we can't climb;   noth - in' keeps us down.

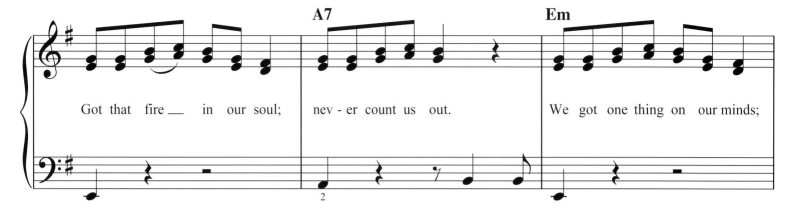

Got that fire __ in our soul; nev - er count us out. We got one thing on our minds;

call it vic - to - ry. Yeah, that's where we're head - ed and we know how to get it.

We were made for this. There's noth-ing we can't __ do. __ We came to play, we're here to stay __

__ and win the day __ 'cause we were made for this. Did - n't come here to __ lose. __

D　　　　　　　　　**A**　　　　　　　**N.C.**

_____ We came to play, we're here to stay, _____ what's left to say __ when we know noth-ing's gon-na get in our way?

Em

No!　So get up　　out of our way, we're fi-red up,　we're fi-red up,　we're fi-red up!
No!　Come on, let me hear　you say, we're fi-red up,　we're fi-red up,　we're fi-red up!

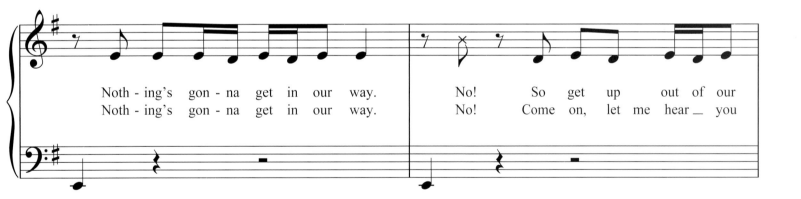

Noth-ing's gon-na get in our way.　　No!　So get up　　out of our
Noth-ing's gon-na get in our way.　　No!　Come on, let me hear __ you

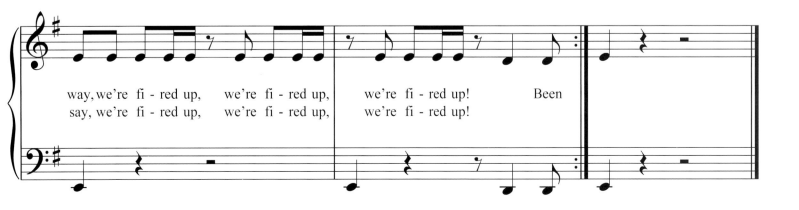

way, we're fi-red up,　we're fi-red up,　we're fi-red up!　　Been
say, we're fi-red up,　we're fi-red up,　we're fi-red up!

OUR YEAR

from *ZOMBIES*

Written by JACK KUGELL,
HANNA JONES and MATT WONG

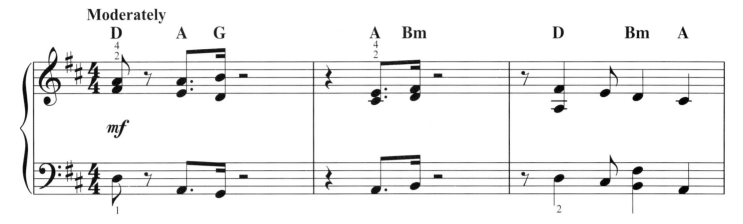

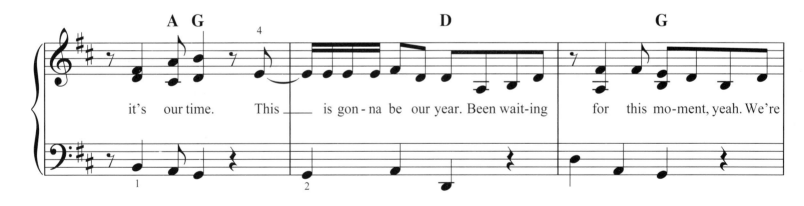

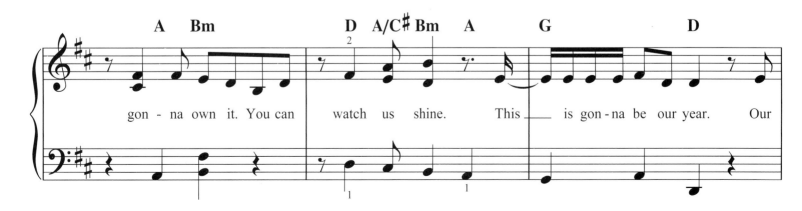

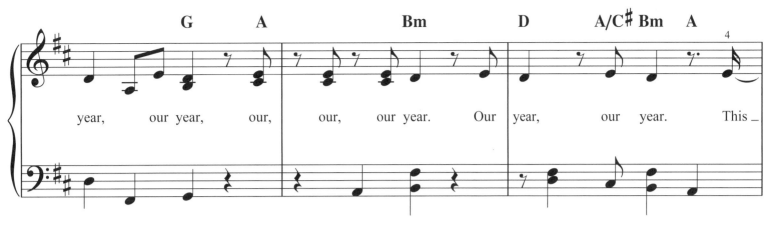

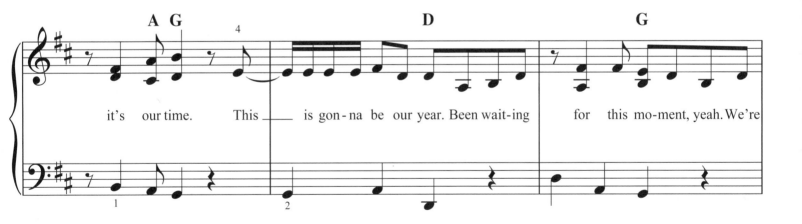

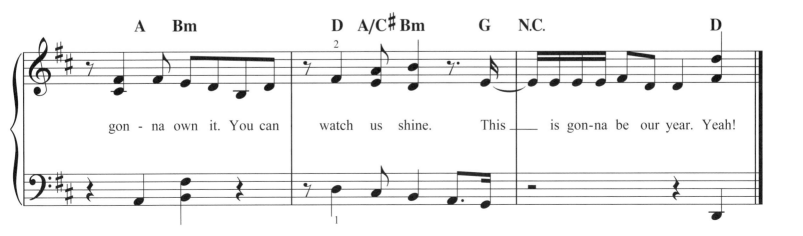

STAND
from *ZOMBIES*

Written by
MATTHEW TISHLER

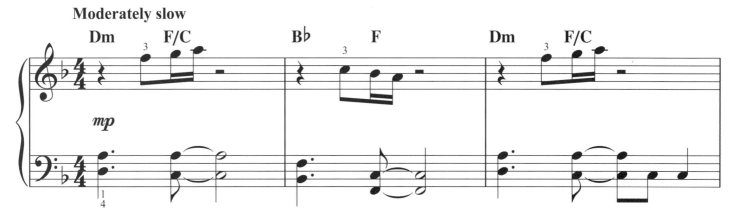

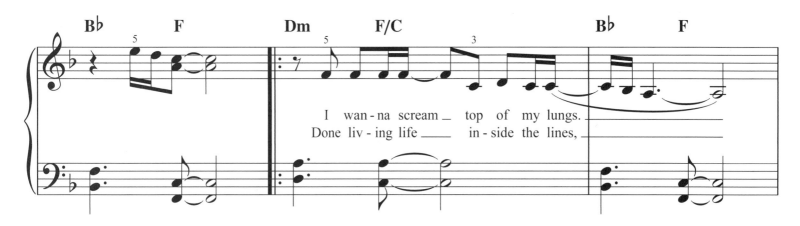

I wan-na scream ___ top of my lungs.
Done liv-ing life ___ in-side the lines,

Not sit-ting back, ___ won't hold my tongue. ___ No!
fol-low-ing the rules ___ and play-ing nice, ___ yeah.

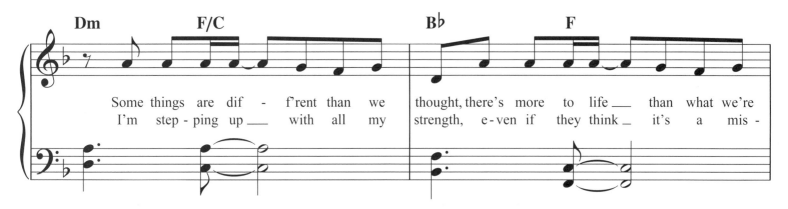

Some things are dif-f'rent than we thought, there's more to life ___ than what we're
I'm step-ping up ___ with all my strength, e-ven if they think ___ it's a mis-

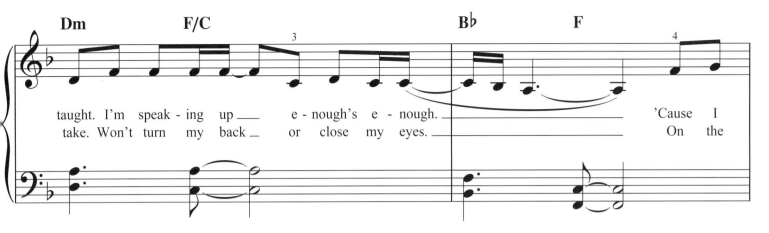

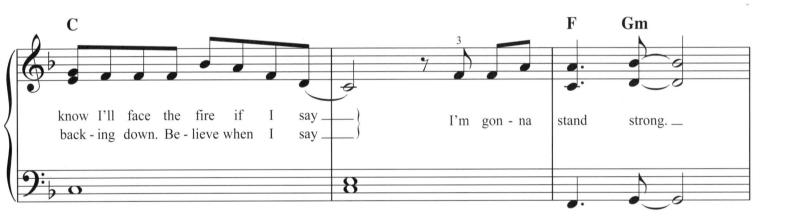

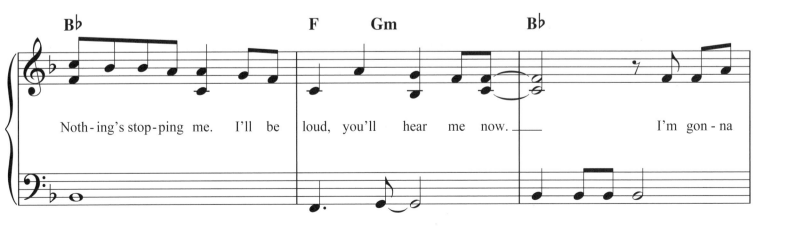

stand tall, ___ take it to the top. I'll be free; can't bring me down. ___

___ So I'll rise, ___ won't turn back. I won't hide ___ who I am. ___

___ I'm gon - na stand.

stand. Yeah, I'm gon - na stand. Oh. ___

13

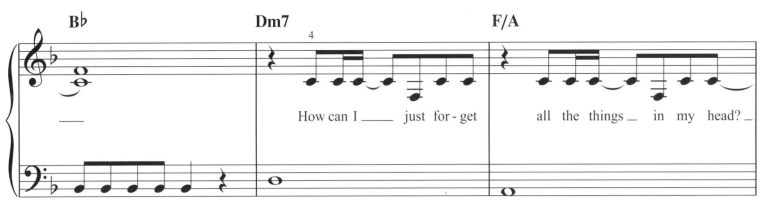

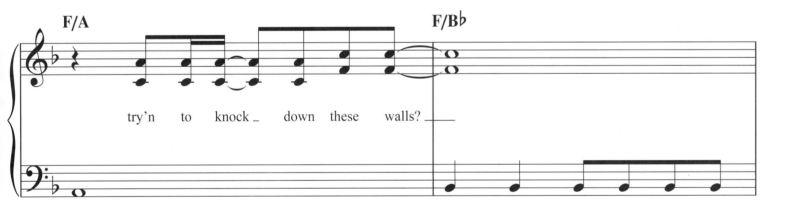

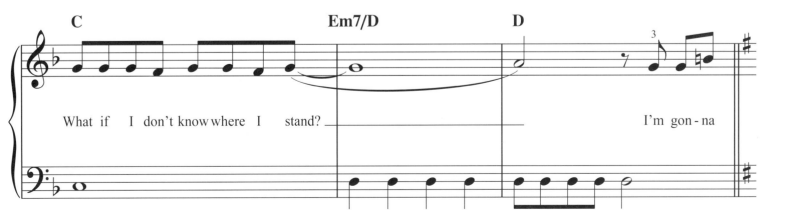

14

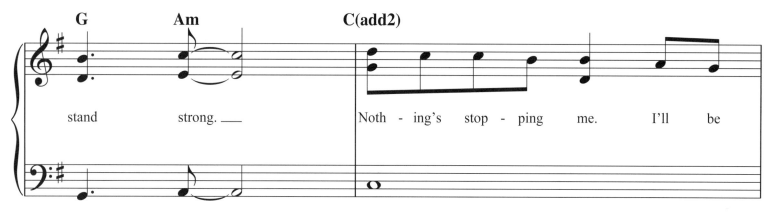

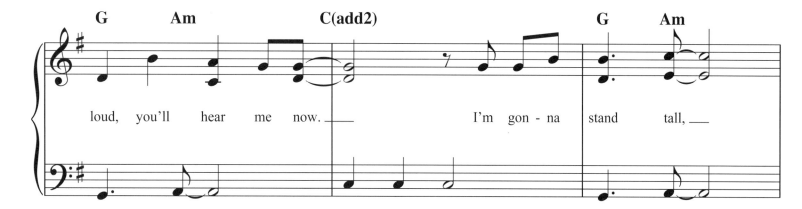

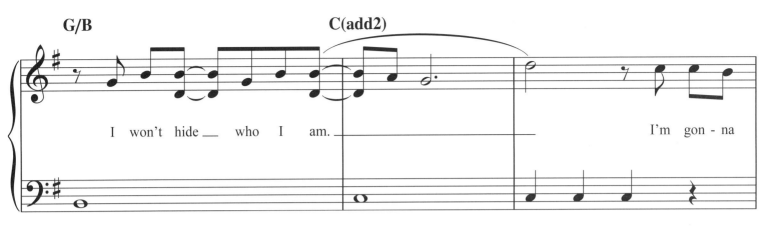

SOMEDAY

from ZOMBIES

Written by DUSTIN BURNETT
and PAULA WINGER

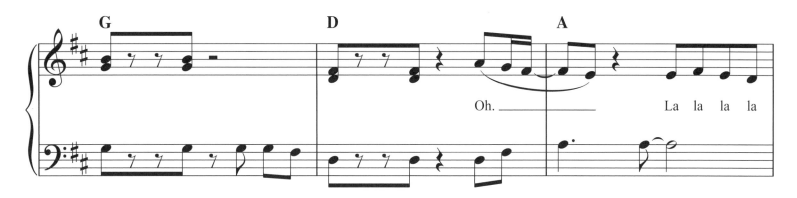

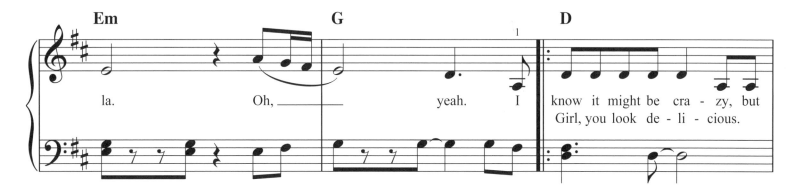

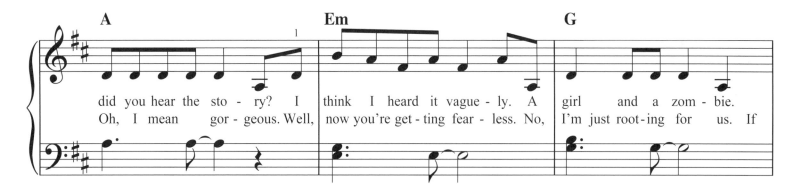

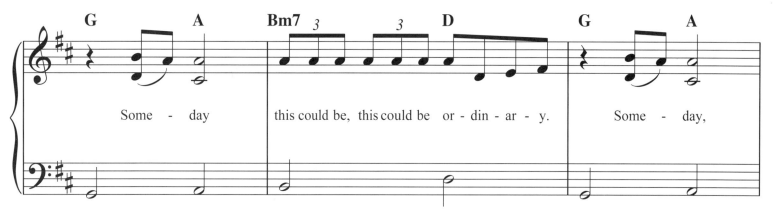

Some - day   this could be, this could be or - din - ar - y.   Some - day,

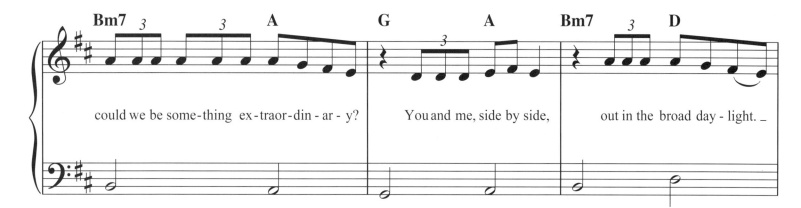

could we be some-thing ex-traor-din - ar - y?   You and me, side by side,   out in the broad day - light. _

If they _ laugh, we'll   say   we're gon-na be some - day.   We're gon-na be some-

day. Some - day, some - day. _   We're gon-na be some - day.

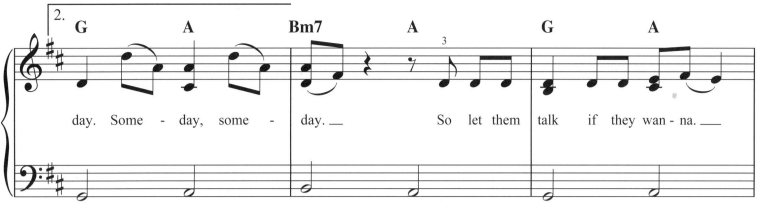

day. Some - day, some - day. ___ So let them talk if they wan - na. ___

Let them talk if they're gon - na. ___ We're gon - na

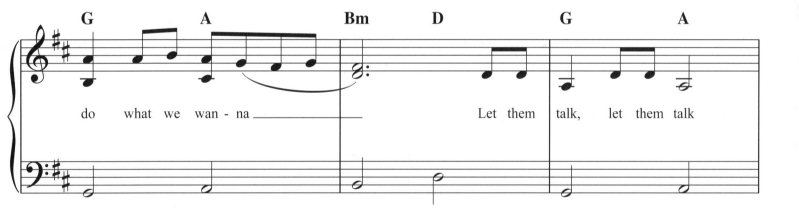

do what we wan - na ___ Let them talk, let them talk

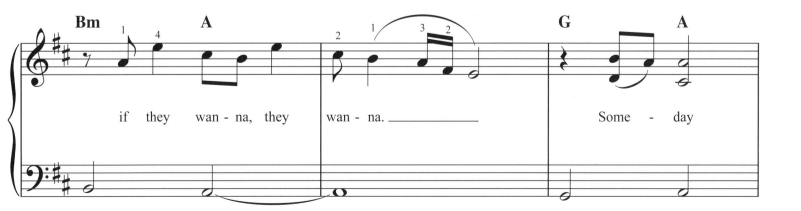

if they wan - na, they wan - na. ___ Some - day

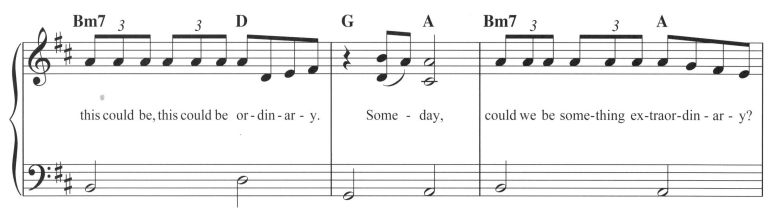

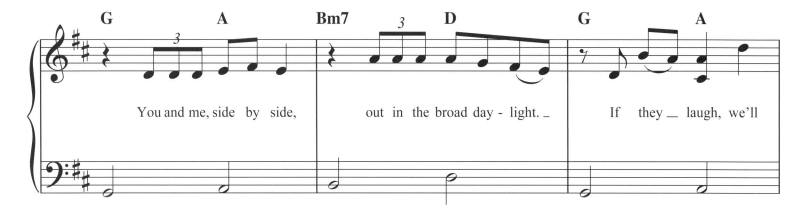

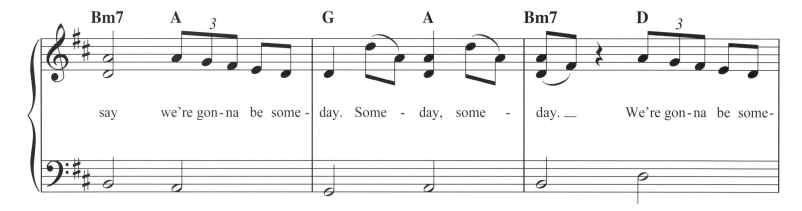

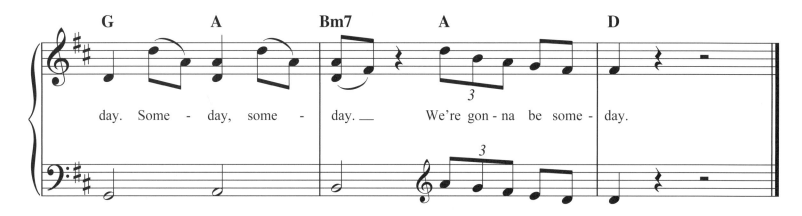

FLESH & BONE

from *ZOMBIES 2*

Written by TOVA LITVIN
and DOUG ROCKWELL

Moving along

N.C.   Dm

Hear it get-ting loud - er? A
Strand - ed at the bot - tom, but

F/C

call for rev - o - lu - tion. Yeah, we
we're more than a whis - per. No, we'll

came for what was ou - rs, it's
nev - er be for - got - ten. Our

C

time for res - ti - tu - tion. We'll pro -
blood's thick - er than sil - ver. Yeah, when

tect our own, take back the stone. No,
world's col - lide, it's do or die. So

G/B

hu - man na - ture can - not hold us
tell me, is it wrong to stand your

down. ___
ground? ___

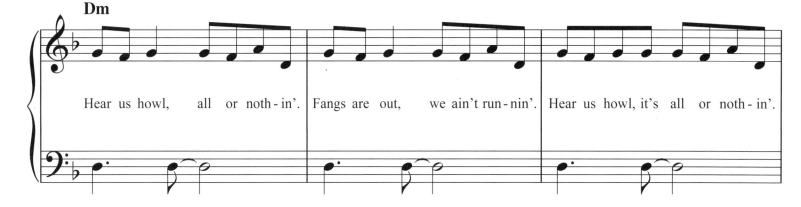

Hear us howl, all or noth-in'. Fangs are out, we ain't run-nin'. Hear us howl, it's all or noth-in'.

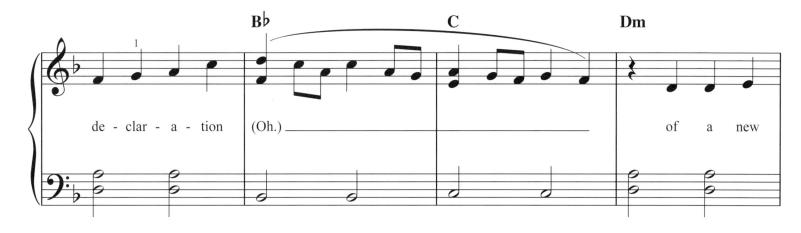

(Oh.) _____ This is a

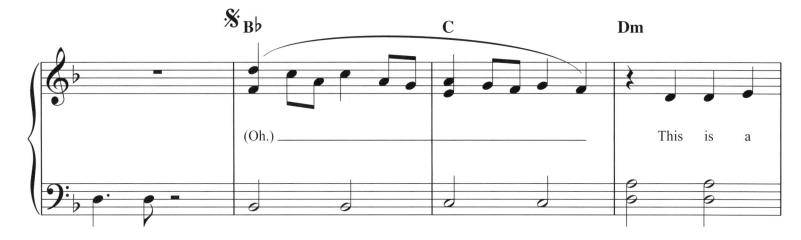

de - clar - a - tion (Oh.) _____ of a new

gen - er - a - tion. It's now or nev - er. We're in this to - geth - er. We'll

fight through the highs and the lows. No, we won't break. We're more than flesh and bone.

The world has gone cra-zy and no one seems to lis-ten. Got-ta
No more hes-i-ta-tion! It's time we start to re-al-ize with

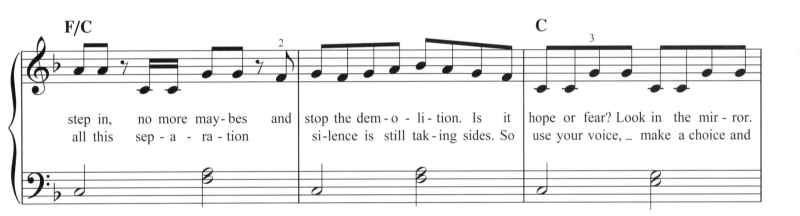

step in, no more may-bes and stop the dem-o-li-tion. Is it hope or fear? Look in the mir-ror.
all this sep-a-ra-tion si-lence is still tak-ing sides. So use your voice, __ make a choice and

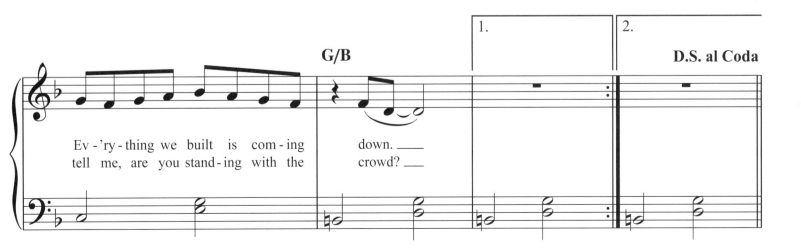

Ev-'ry-thing we built is com-ing down. __
tell me, are you stand-ing with the crowd? __

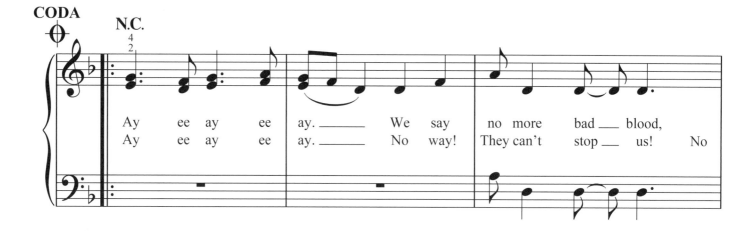

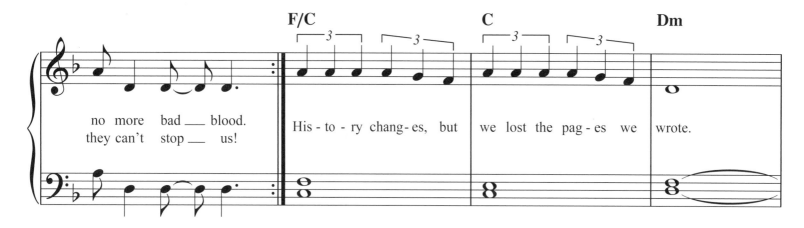

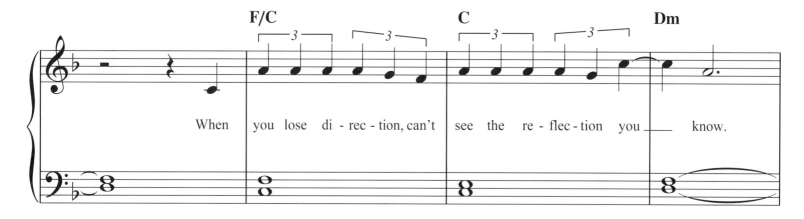

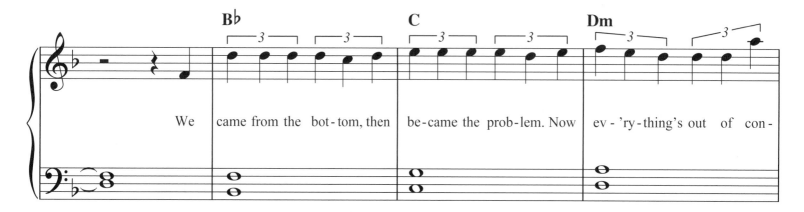

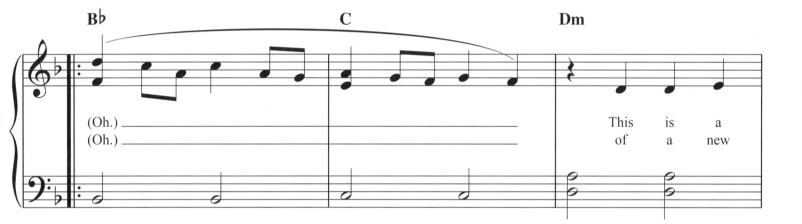

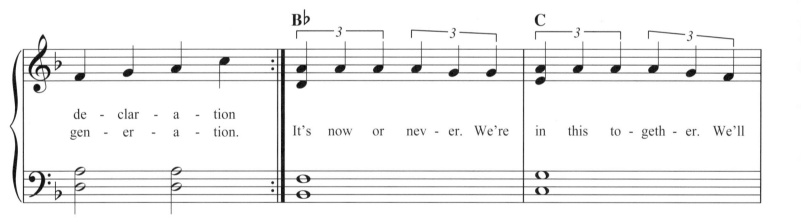

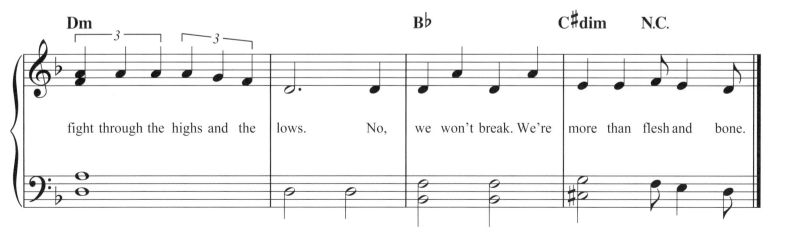

LIKE THE ZOMBIES DO

from *ZOMBIES 2*

Written by ANTONINA ARMATO,
TIM JAMES PRICE, THOMAS ARMATO STURGES,
and ADAM SCHMALHOLZ

With a beat

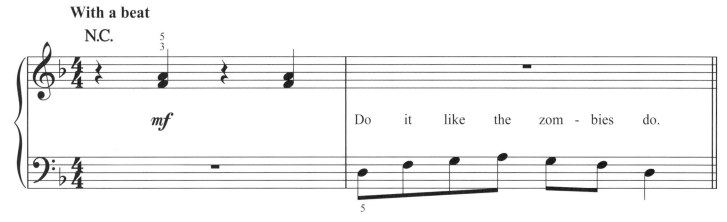

Do it like the zom - bies do.

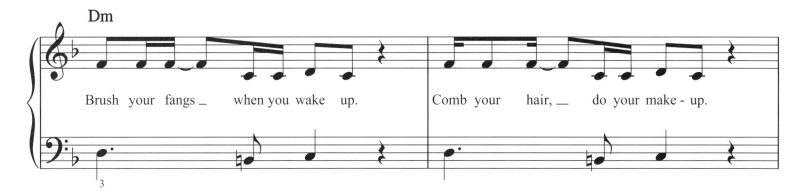

Brush your fangs __ when you wake up. Comb your hair, __ do your make - up.

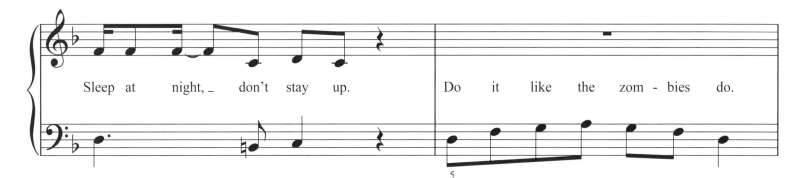

Sleep at night, __ don't stay up. Do it like the zom - bies do.

Don't stand out __ when you're fit - tin' in. When in doubt, __ do the op - po - site. Don't

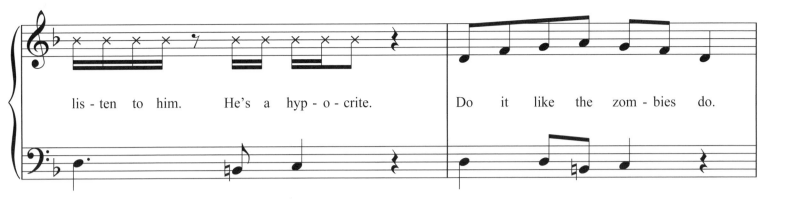

Why should we change? They should be like us. Yeah,

he may eat brains, but he's got no guts. He's gone in-sane. Yeah, he's

act-ing nuts! Come on, we've got moves to bust! Whoa!

Do it! Do it! Do it like the zom-bies do. Do it! Do it! Do it

like the zom-bies do. Do it! Do it! Do it! Do what you want to do. __

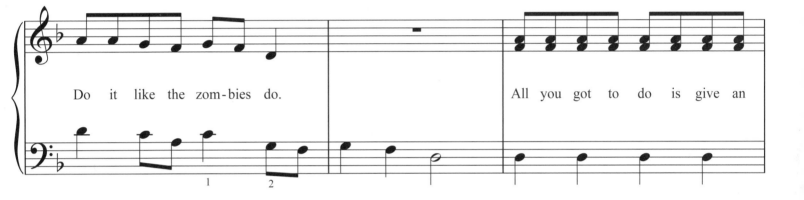

Do it like the zom-bies do. All you got to do is give an

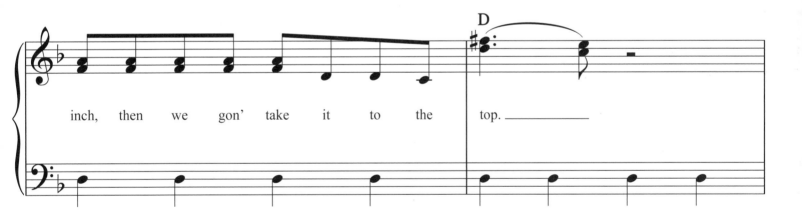

inch, then we gon' take it to the top. _____

Do it like the zom-bies do. Don't stop. _____ Do it like the zom-bies do.

WE OWN THE NIGHT

from *ZOMBIES 2*

Written by ANTONINA ARMATO,
TIM JAMES PRICE, THOMAS ARMATO STURGES,
and ADAM SCHMALHOLZ

Moderately fast

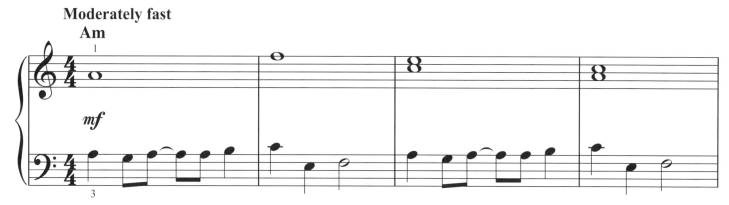

No one's catch-ing me un-less I wan-na be caught. I'm danc-ing in the shad-ows ain't no

leash when I walk. It's great to feel in-vin-ci-ble, it's great to feel a-live. My

ap - pe - tite's in - sa - tia - ble there's no - where it can hide.

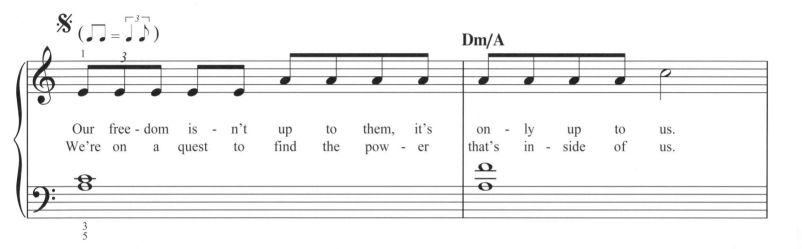

Our free - dom is - n't up to them, it's on - ly up to us.
We're on a quest to find the pow - er that's in - side of us.

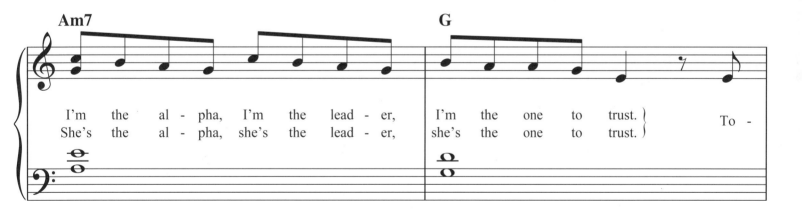

I'm the al - pha, I'm the lead - er, I'm the one to trust. To -
She's the al - pha, she's the lead - er, she's the one to trust.

geth - er we do what - ev - er it takes. We're in this pack for life. A -

34

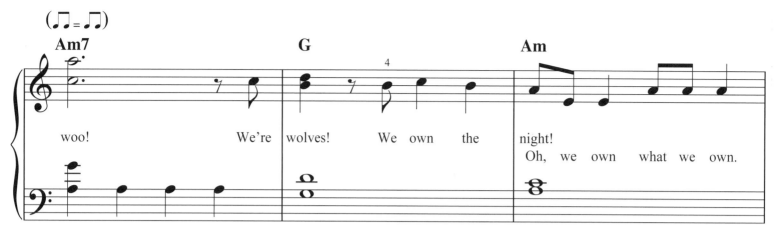

I'm pick-ing up the scent. It seems we're on the right track. The

moon-light's on the roof-tops. The wind is at our backs. We're liv-ing in the shad-ows. We're

D.S. al Coda

liv-ing for the chase. Our leg-a-cy is in our sights so let's pick up the pace!

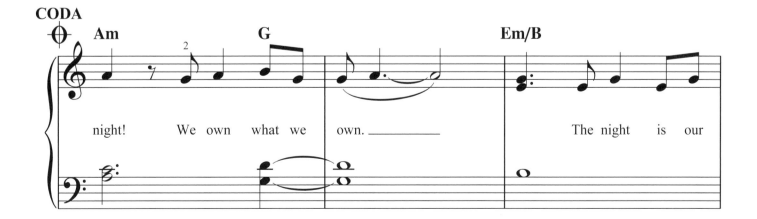

CODA

night! We own what we own. _____ The night is our

36

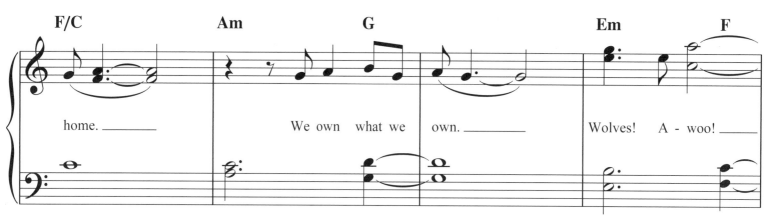

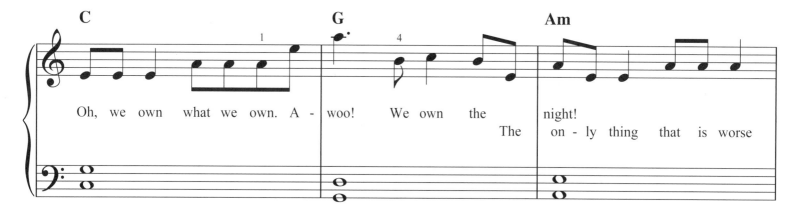

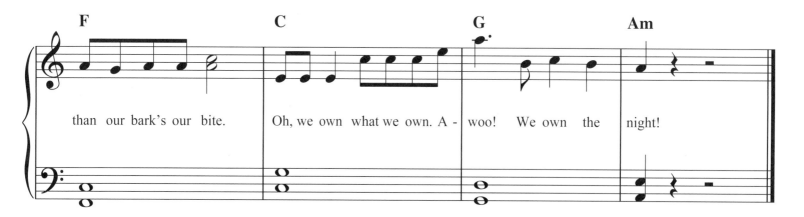

WE GOT THIS
from *ZOMBIES 2*

Written by MITCH ALLAN,
CHANTRY JOHNSON and MICHELLE ZARLENGA

Moderately fast

Oh Ad - di - son, my love, __ "Gar gar ga - za" for - ev - er! We

pull the strings, _ we run the show. _ We're bet - ter than ev - er, bet - ter than ev - er! We're

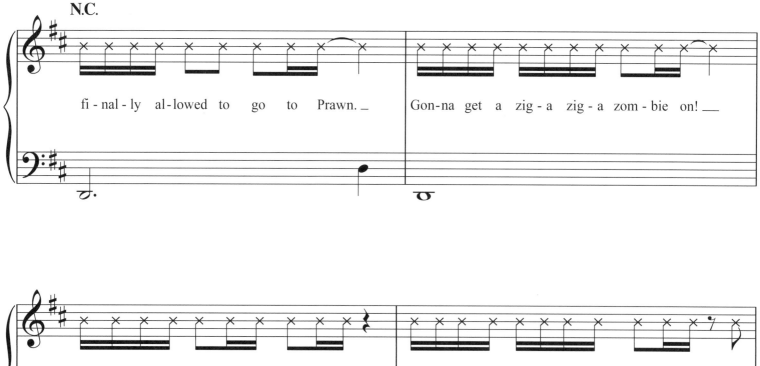

N.C.

fi - nal - ly al - lowed to go to Prawn. _ Gon - na get a zig - a zig - a zom - bie on! __

Count - ing down the days I've been keep - ing track. Kind - a wish - ing Ad - di - son would write me back Im-

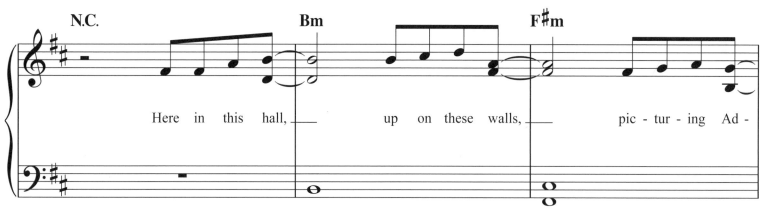

Here in this hall, __ up on these walls, __ pic - tur - ing Ad -

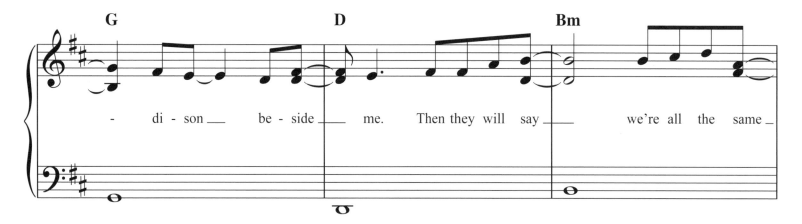

- di - son __ be - side __ me. Then they will say __ we're all the same __

__ and they can see __ the life __ in - side __ me. Oh,

what's it gon - na take, what's it gon - na take? What's it gon - na take, what's it gon - na take, what's it gon - na

EXCEPTIONAL ZED
from *ZOMBIES 3*

Written by MITCH ALLAN,
CHANTRY JOHNSON and MICHELLE ZARLENGA

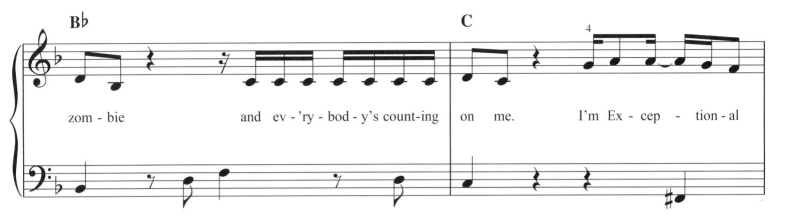

zom - bie and ev -'ry - bod - y's count-ing on me. I'm Ex - cep - tion - al

Zed to all my fam -'ly and friends. So I just got - ta for-

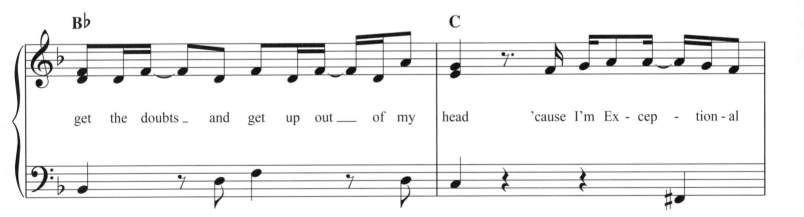

get the doubts and get up out of my head 'cause I'm Ex - cep - tion - al

Zed. I'm out here do - ing my best. To - day, I got - ta be

good to go ___ so I'll say it o - ver a - gain: I'm Ex - cep - tion - al Zed. *I guess.*

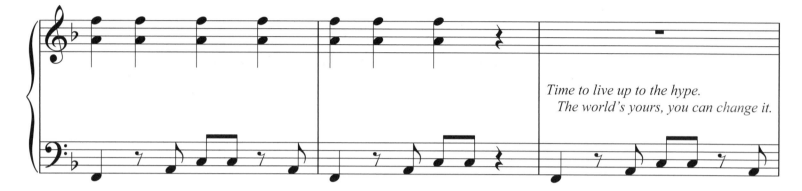

Time to live up to the hype.
The world's yours, you can change it.

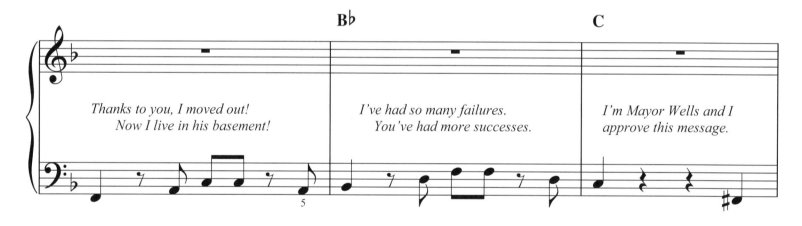

Thanks to you, I moved out!
Now I live in his basement!

I've had so many failures.
You've had more successes.

I'm Mayor Wells and I
approve this message.

Am I really that great? In case you forgot,
you've changed the whole school!
Whether I like it or not.

You're smart, you work hard,
you can make it all happen.

48

AIN'T NO DOUBT ABOUT IT

from *ZOMBIES 3*

Written by JOSH CUMBEE
and JORDAN POWERS

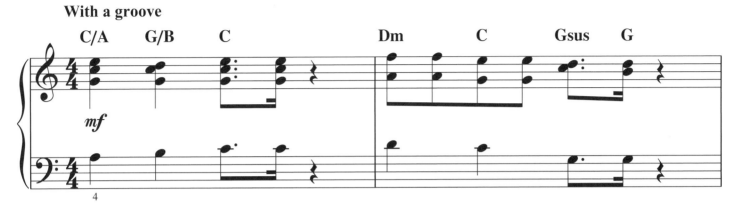

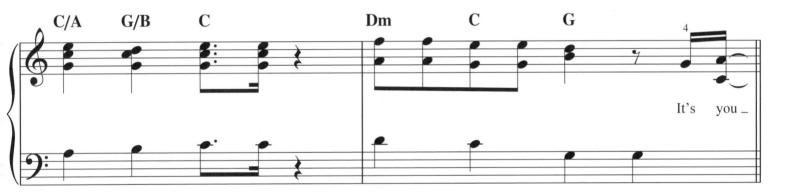

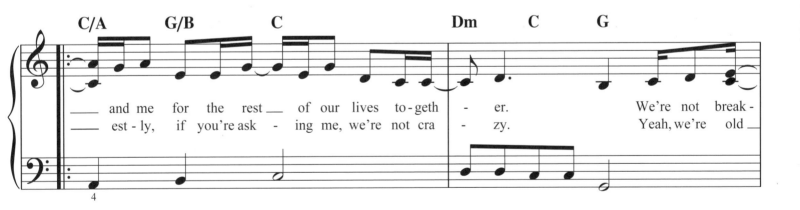

_ and me for the rest _ of our lives to-geth - er. We're not break-
_ est - ly, if you're ask - ing me, we're not cra - zy. Yeah, we're old _

- ing up, we're not fall - ing out, we won't _ change. Liv - ing per-
_ e-nough to know we're _ in love. That's no _ lie. If you prom-

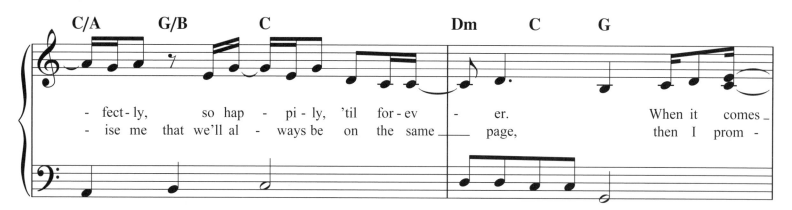

-fect- ly, so hap - pi - ly, 'til for - ev - er. When it comes
-ise me that we'll al - ways be on the same page, then I prom -

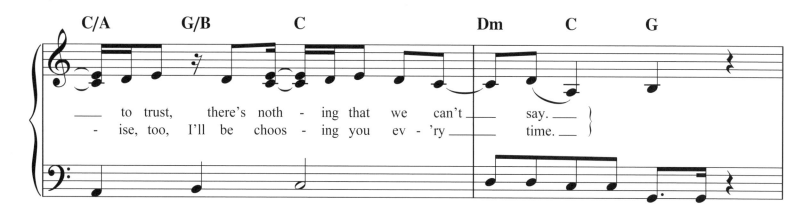

to trust, there's noth - ing that we can't say.
- ise, too, I'll be choos - ing you ev - 'ry time.

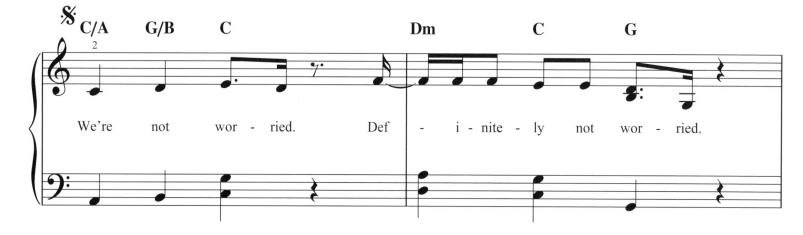

We're not wor - ried. Def - i - nite - ly not wor - ried.

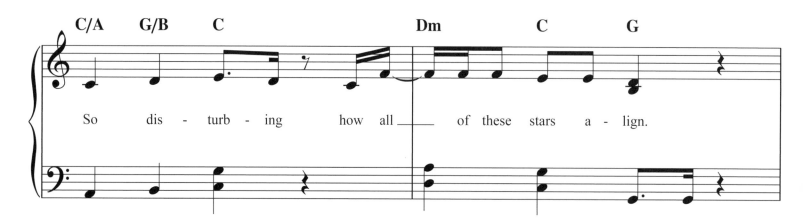

So dis - turb - ing how all of these stars a - lign.

We're not ner - vous. We're to - tal - ly un - con - cerned with

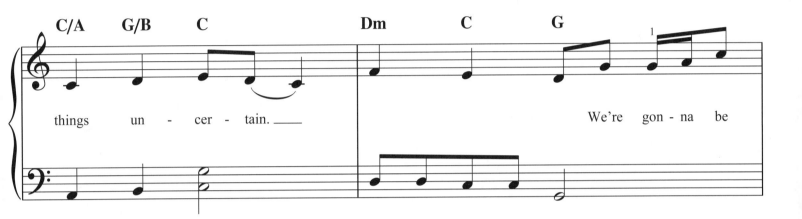

things un - cer - tain. _____ We're gon - na be

fine, so fine. Ain't no doubt a - bout it! It's work - in' out

right, all right. All I'm think - ing 'bout is how

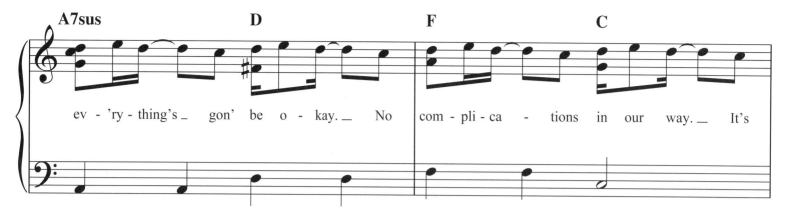

ev - 'ry - thing's _ gon' be o - kay. _ No com - pli - ca - tions in our way. _ It's

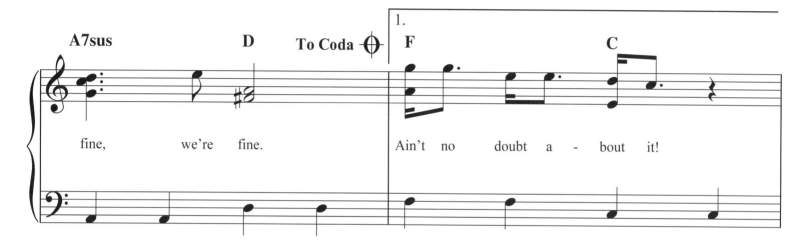

fine, we're fine. Ain't no doubt a - bout it!

Hon - Ain't no doubt a - bout it!

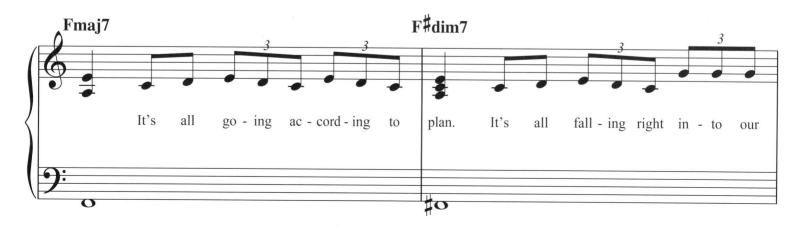

It's all go - ing ac - cord - ing to plan. It's all fall - ing right in - to our

I'M FINALLY ME

from *ZOMBIES 3*

Written by KARI KIMMEL
and CAS WEINBREN

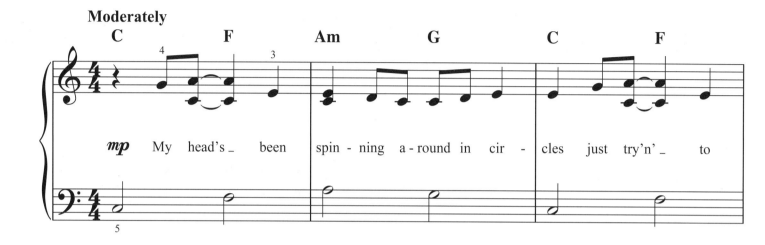

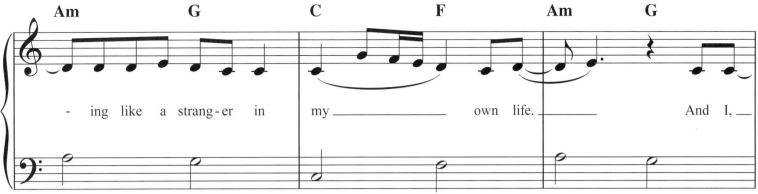

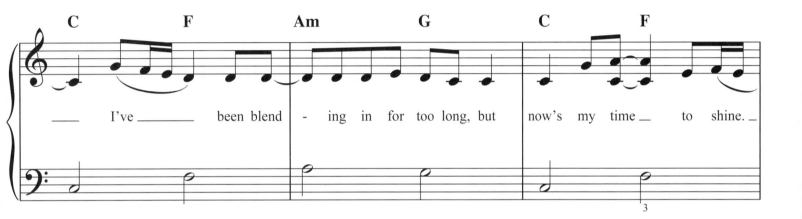

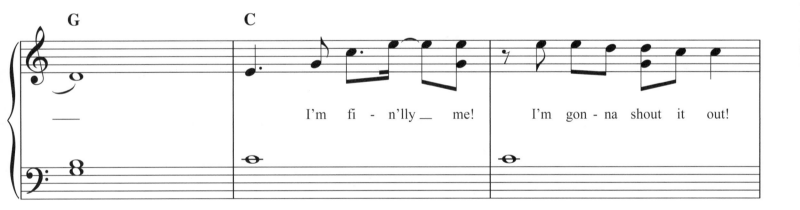

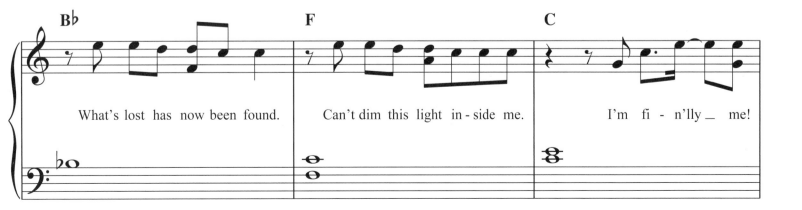

No long-er gon-na hide.   I'm just like dy-na-mite.   Can't hold me back, now I'm free. _

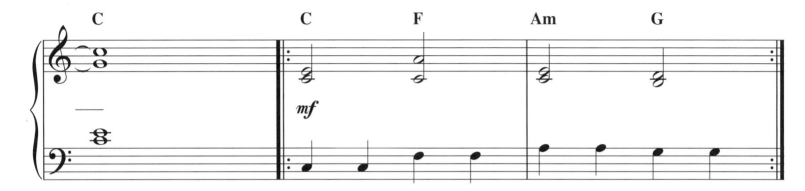

I'm strong - er   now, more than ev-er be - fore. Noth-ing ___ can

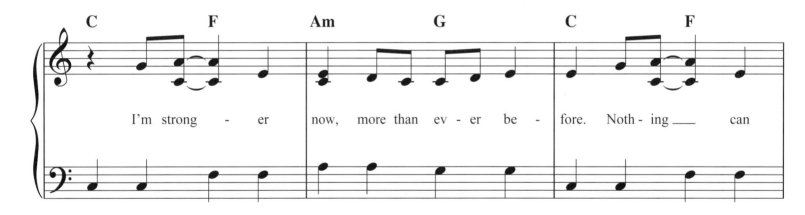

hold me back.   I'm la - ser   fo - cused, con - fi - dent and so

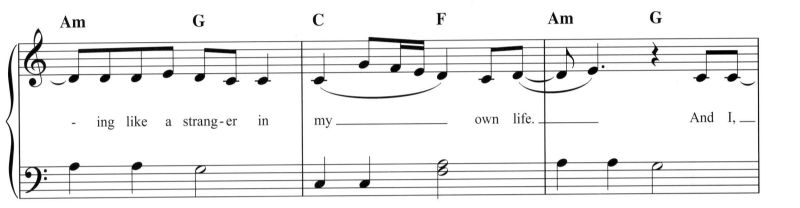

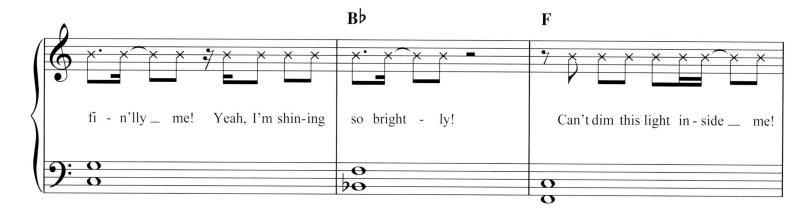

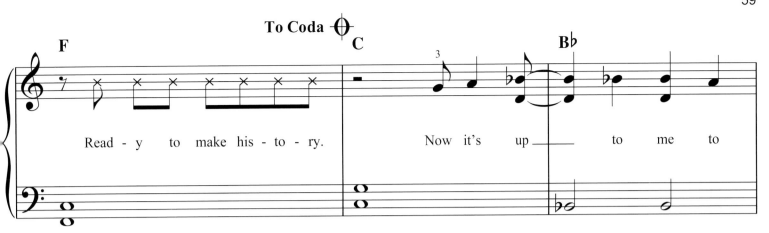

Ready to make his-to-ry. Now it's up to me to

prove to ev-'ry-one we will rise

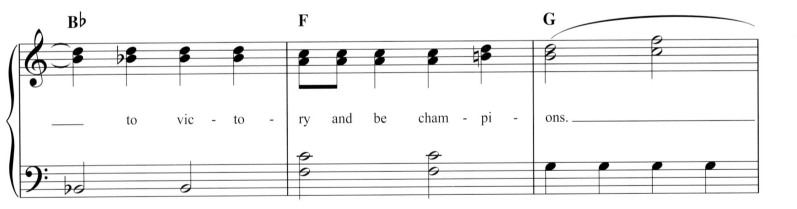

to vic-to-ry and be cham-pi-ons.

D.S. al Coda

I'm fi-n'lly me!

CODA

N.C.

mp *pp*

NOTHING BUT LOVE

from *ZOMBIES 3*

Written by
CHEN NEEMAN

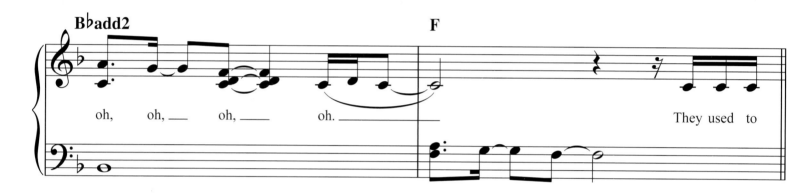

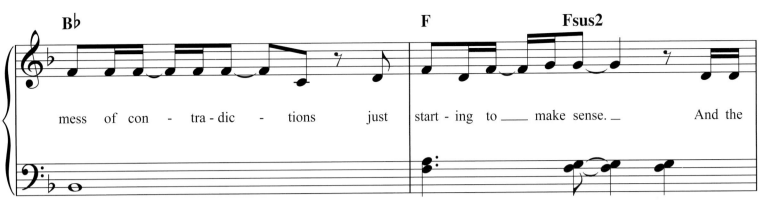

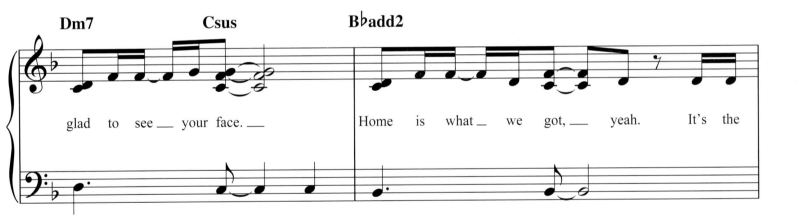

To Coda

love for ___ you, ___ love for ___ you! ___ Noth-in' but love. Woo __ woo. ___

Noth-in' but love. Woo __ woo. ___ Noth-in' but

love. We still own __ the night ___ and shar - ing it, ___ that's new. But the

stars shine so much bright- er, now I'm shar - ing them __ with you. ___

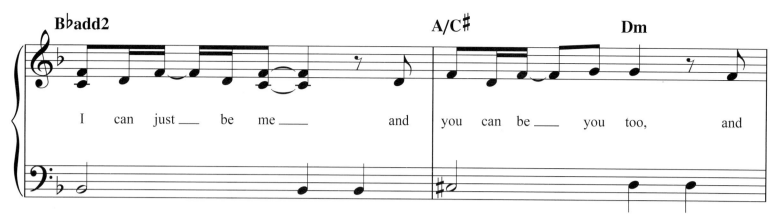

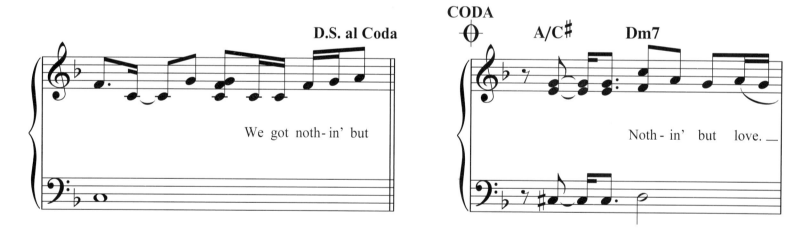